STEP-BY-STEP

Recipes with Yogurt

STEP-BY-STEP

Recipes with Yogurt

PAMELA WESTLAND

‖ •PARRAGON• ‖

First published in Great Britain in 1994 by
Parragon Book Service Ltd
Unit 13-17, Avonbridge Trading Estate
Atlantic Road
Avonmouth
Bristol BS11 9QD

ISBN 1 85813 654 7

Printed in Italy

Acknowledgements:

Design & DTP: Pedro & Frances Prá-Lopez / Kingfisher Design
Art Direction: Pedro Prá-Lopez
Managing Editor: Alexa Stace
Special Photography: Amanda Heywood
Home Economist: Louise Pickford
Stylist: Marion Price
Photograph page 75: Clive Streeter
Step-by-step Photographs page 74: Karl Adamson

Gas Hob supplied by New World Domestic Appliances Ltd
Photographs on pages 6, 14, 26, 34 & 54: By courtesy of ZEFA

Note:
Cup measurements in this book are for American cups. Tablespoons are assumed to be 15ml.
All eggs are size 2 unless otherwise stated

Contents

First Courses

Yogurt has a delicious contribution to make in a wide range of
first courses. You can use it in place of cream in savoury
mousses and cheesecakes, to complement flavours as diverse as
those of Jerusalem artichokes and smoked salmon. You can
combine yogurt with light chicken stock and beaten eggs
to make a Middle-Eastern-style soup, or garnish a wide range
of creamy vegetable or fish soups with a swirl of yogurt.

You can also serve a selection of yogurt salads as a first course with
style, offering, for example, avocado sauce and cucumber
salad with crisps and crackers, breadsticks and fresh vegetable
crudités. Or you can toss mixed leaf and vegetable salads
with a piquant yogurt and lemon or vinaigrette dressing.
In contrast, try serving melt-in-the-mouth fried yogurt cheese
(from the recipe on page 77) with a small side salad
and plenty of warm, crusty bread.

Opposite: *Healthy drinks and
snacks are quick and easy to
whip up with yogurt, and
assorted fruits and nuts.*

ARTICHOKE MOUSSE

Artichoke hearts have a characteristic tanginess, well complemented by a colourful (bell) pepper salad in this stylish first course.

STEP 2

SERVES 6

1 x 425 g/15 oz can artichoke hearts
150 ml/¼ pint/⅔ cup condensed consommé
juice of ½ orange
large pinch of grated nutmeg
4 tbsp warm water
1 sachet gelatine
2 egg whites
300 ml/½ pint/1¼ cups Greek-style yogurt
salt and pepper

SALAD:
3 large (bell) peppers, various colours
3 tbsp olive oil
juice of ½ orange
2 tbsp natural yogurt
2 tbsp chopped parsley

1 Drain the artichoke hearts, and reserve the liquid. Place the hearts in a food processor with 3 tablespoons of liquid, the consommé, orange juice and nutmeg. Process until finely chopped but not puréed. Season, pour into a large bowl and set aside.

2 Pour the water into a small bowl and sprinkle on the gelatine. Place the bowl in a pan of simmering water and stir until the crystals have dissolved, then remove and set aside to cool.

3 Whisk the egg whites until they are stiff but not dry.

4 When the gelatine is syrupy and on the point of setting, blend well into the artichoke mixture. Stir in the yogurt, using an up-and-over movement, until thoroughly blended. Fold in the egg whites, using a metal spoon. Pour into a wetted ring mould or 6 individual moulds, cover and chill for at least 3 hours or until set.

5 Heat the grill (broiler) to high and sear the (bell) peppers close to the heat until evenly blackened all round. Plunge into cold water and as soon as they are cool enough to handle peel off the skins. Core and seed, cut into thick strips and leave to cool.

6 Beat together the olive oil, orange juice and yogurt and season. Pour over the (bell) peppers and stir in the chopped parsley.

7 Run a knife around the inside of the moulds and invert on to serving plates, shaking the mould to release it. Pile the salad into the centre of the mould and serve chilled, with crispy bread rolls or black rye bread.

STEP 4

STEP 5

STEP 7

STEP 2a

STEP 2b

STEP 3

STEP 5

SMOKED SALMON CHEESECAKE

This rich, creamy cheesecake makes a memorable first course for a special occasion. You can also serve it as a lunch or supper dish,

SERVES 6

90 g/3 oz/6 tbsp butter
200 g/7 oz water biscuits (cookies), crushed
1 tbsp sesame seeds
salt and pepper

FILLING:
175 g/6 oz smoked salmon pieces, roughly chopped
grated rind and juice of 1 lemon
250 g/8 oz/1 cup full fat soft cheese
2 eggs, separated
150 ml/¼ pint/⅔ cup natural yogurt
freshly ground black pepper
4 tbsp warm water
1 sachet gelatine

TOPPING:
150 ml/¼ pint/⅔ cup Greek-style yogurt
4 thin slices lemon
a few sprigs of fresh dill
12 whole prawns (shrimp) (optional)

1 Grease a loose-bottomed 20 cm/ 8 in cake tin (pan).

2 Melt the butter in a pan. Remove from the heat, stir in the biscuit (cookie) crumbs and sesame seeds and season. Press the mixture evenly over the base of the prepared tin (pan) and chill.

3 Process the smoked salmon and lemon juice briefly in a food processor, then turn into a bowl and beat in the cheese, egg yolks and yogurt. Season well with pepper.

4 Pour the water into a small bowl and sprinkle on the gelatine. Place the bowl in a pan of simmering water and stir until the crystals have dissolved. Remove from the heat and set aside to cool. When the gelatine is syrupy and on the point of setting, pour into the salmon mixture and stir to blend thoroughly.

5 Whisk the egg whites until stiff but not dry. Using a metal spoon, fold them into the fish mixture until they are well blended. Pour the filling into the prepared tin (pan) and level the surface. Chill for 3-4 hours until set.

6 Lift the cheesecake out of the tin (pan), keeping it on the metal base, and place on a flat serving dish. Spread the yogurt evenly over the top or place in a piping bag and pipe swirls. Cut the lemon slices in quarters and arrange in pairs to form butterfly shapes around the rim of the cheesecake . Arrange the dill sprigs on top and garnish with the prawns (shrimp), if using. Serve chilled.

YOGURT & SPINACH SOUP

Whole young spinach leaves add vibrant colour to this unusual soup.

STEP 1

STEP 3

STEP 4

STEP 5

SERVES 4

600 ml/1 pint/2½ cups chicken stock
60 g/2 oz/4 tbsp long-grain rice, rinsed and
*   drained*
4 tbsp water
1 tbsp cornflour (cornstarch)
600 ml/1 pint/2½ cups natural yogurt
juice of 1 lemon
3 egg yolks, lightly beaten
350 g/12 oz young spinach leaves, washed
*   and drained*
salt and pepper

1 Pour the stock into a large pan, season and bring to the boil. Add the rice and simmer for 10 minutes, until barely cooked. Remove from the heat.

2 Pour the water into a small bowl and sift the cornflour (cornstarch) into it. Stir to make a thin, smooth paste.

3 Pour the yogurt into a second pan and stir in the cornflour (cornstarch) mixture. Set the pan over a low heat and bring the yogurt slowly to the boil, stirring with a wooden spoon in one direction only. This will stabilize the yogurt and prevent it from separating or curdling on contact with the hot stock. When the yogurt has reached boiling point, stand the pan on a heat diffuser and leave to simmer slowly for 10 minutes. Remove the pan from the heat and allow the mixture to cool slightly before stirring in the beaten egg yolks.

4 Pour the yogurt mixture into the stock, stir in the lemon juice and stir to blend thoroughly. Keep the soup warm, but do not allow it to boil.

5 Blanch the spinach leaves in a large pan of boiling, salted water for 2-3 minutes until they begin to soften but have not collapsed. Tip the spinach into a colander, drain well and stir it into the soup. Taste the soup and adjust the seasoning if necesary. Serve in wide shallow soup plates, with hot, crusty bread.

TO STABILIZE YOGURT

When stabilizing yogurt in the way described, it is important to stir it slowly and rhythmically in one direction only. Do not cover the pan, because any drops of condensation falling into the yogurt could cause it to separate. And do not be tempted to swish it about in first one direction and then the other.

CHAPTER TWO

Fish

Yogurt has a subtle and sometimes undetected part to play
in fish dishes of all kinds. In the dish of Baked Red Snapper,
for example (page 20), which has the aroma and flavour
of Greek island cookery, it is yogurt that harmonizes
the fragrances and flavours of the herbs,
garlic and vegetables.

And in the accompanying salad, it is yogurt which neutralizes
any sharpness there may be in fresh vegetable leaves.
Yogurt also plays a key role in smooth tangy dishes,
such as Shrimp Curry &Fruit Sauce (page 25), and
gives a new slant on poaching salmon steaks.
In fact, yogurt is the perfect partner for fish –
try the Fish & Seafood Chowder on
page 22 and taste the difference.

Opposite: *A Sicilian fisherman
mends his nets in the port of
Palermo. Yogurt makes a very
good partner for fish of all
kinds, providing the basis for
smooth, subtly-flavoured
sauces.*

STEP 1

STEP 2

STEP 3

STEP 4

POACHED SALMON

Salmon steaks, poached in a well-flavoured stock and served with a piquant sauce, make a delicious summer lunch or supper dish.

SERVES 4

1 small onion, sliced
1 small carrot, sliced
1 stick celery, sliced
1 bay leaf
pared rind and juice of ½ orange
a few stalks of parsley
salt
5-6 black peppercorns
750 ml/1¼ pints/3 cups water
4 salmon steaks, about 350 g/12 oz each
salad leaves, to serve
lemon twists, to garnish

SAUCE:

1 large avocado, peeled, halved and stoned
125 ml/4 fl oz/½ cup Greek-style yogurt
grated zest and juice of ½ orange
black pepper
a few drops of hot red pepper sauce

1 Put the onion, carrot, celery, bay leaf, orange rind, orange juice, parsley stalks, salt and peppercorns in a pan just large enough to take the salmon steaks in a single layer. Pour on the water, cover the pan and bring to the boil. Simmer the stock for 20 minutes.

2 Arrange the salmon steaks in the pan, return the stock to the boil and simmer for 3 minutes. Cover the pan, remove from the heat and leave the salmon to cool in the stock.

3 To make the sauce, roughly chop the avocado and place it in a blender or food processor with the yogurt, orange zest and orange juice. Process to make a smooth sauce, then season to taste with salt, pepper and hot pepper sauce.

4 Remove the salmon steaks from the stock (reserve it to make fish soup or a sauce), skin them and pat dry with paper towels.

5 Cover the serving dish with salad leaves, arrange the salmon steaks on top and spoon a little of the sauce into the centre of each one. Garnish the fish with lemon twists, and serve the remaining sauce separately.

ACCOMPANIMENT

The salmon could be served with New Potato Salad (see page 76) as an ideal accompaniment.

STEP 3

STEP 4a

STEP 4b

STEP 5

QUENELLES & WATERCRESS SAUCE

The quenelles, made from a thick purée of fish and yogurt, can be prepared well in advance and stored in the refrigerator.

SERVES 4

750 g/1½ lb white fish fillets, such as cod, coley or whiting, skinned
2 small egg whites
½ tsp ground coriander
1 tsp ground mace
150 ml/¼ pint/⅔ cup natural yogurt
1 small onion, sliced
salt and pepper
mixture of boiled Basmati rice and wild rice, to serve

SAUCE:
1 bunch watercress, trimmed
300 ml/½ pint/1¼ cups chicken stock
2 tbsp cornflour (cornstarch)
150 ml/¼ pint/⅔ cup natural yogurt
2 tbsp crème fraîche

1 Cut the fish into pieces and process it in a food processor for about 30 seconds, until it is finely chopped.

2 Add the egg whites to the fish and process for a further 30 seconds until the mixture forms a stiff paste. Add the coriander and mace and season. Add the yogurt and process until well blended. Transfer the mixture to a covered container and chill it for at least 30 minutes.

3 Spoon the mixture into a piping bag, and pipe into sausage shapes about 10 cm/4 in long. Cut off each length with a knife. Alternatively, take rounded dessertspoons of the mixture and shape into ovals, using 2 spoons.

4 Bring about 5 cm/2 in of water to the boil in a frying pan and add the onion for flavouring. Lower the quenelles into the water, using a fish slice or spoon. Cover the pan, keep the water at a gentle rolling boil and poach the quenelles for 8 minutes, turning them once. Remove with a slotted spoon and drain on paper towels.

5 To make the sauce, roughly chop the watercress, reserving a few sprigs for garnish. Process the remainder with the chicken stock until well blended then pour into a small pan. Stir the cornflour (cornstarch) into the yogurt and pour the mixture into the pan. Bring to the boil, stirring. Stir in the crème fraîche, season and remove from the heat. Pour the sauce into a warmed dish and serve it separately.

6 Garnish with the reserved watercress sprigs. Serve with a Basmati rice and wild rice mixture.

STEP 1

STEP 2

STEP 4a

STEP 4b

BAKED RED SNAPPER

*You can substitute other whole fish for the snapper,
or use cutlets of cod or halibut.*

SERVES 4
OVEN: 190°C/375°F/GAS 5

*1 red snapper, sea bream, or other whole
    fish, about 1.25 kg/2 lb, cleaned
juice of 2 limes, or 1 lemon
4-5 sprigs of thyme, lemon thyme or
    parsley
3 tbsp olive oil
1 large onion, chopped
2 garlic cloves, finely chopped
1 x 425 g/14 oz can chopped tomatoes
2 tbsp tomato purée (paste)
2 tbsp red wine vinegar
5 tbsp Greek-style yogurt
2 tbsp chopped parsley
2 tsp dried oregano
6 tbsp dry breadcrumbs
60 g/2 oz/¼ cup yogurt cheese (see page
    77), or feta cheese, crumbled
salt and pepper
lime wedges and dill sprigs, to serve*

SALAD:
*1 small lettuce, thickly sliced
10-12 young spinach leaves, torn
½ small cucumber, sliced and quartered
4 spring onions (scallions), thickly sliced
3 tbsp chopped parsley
2 tbsp olive oil
2 tbsp plain yogurt
1 tbsp red wine vinegar*

1 Wash the fish and dry with paper
towels. Sprinkle the lime or lemon
juice inside and over the fish, and season
well. Place the herbs inside the fish.

2 Heat the oil in a pan and fry the
onion until translucent. Stir in the
garlic and cook for 1 minute, then stir in
the chopped tomatoes, tomato purée
(paste) and wine vinegar. Bring to the
boil and simmer, uncovered, for 5
minutes until it has thickened slightly.

3 Remove the pan from the heat,
allow the sauce to cool a little, then
stir in the yogurt, parsley and oregano.

4 Pour half the sauce into a shallow,
ovenproof dish just large enough to
take the fish. Pour the remainder of the
sauce over it, and sprinkle on the
breadcrumbs. Bake uncovered for 30-35
minutes, until it is firm. Sprinkle the
yogurt cheese or feta over the fish and
serve with lime wedges and dill sprigs.
Serve the salad separately.

5 Arrange the lettuce, spinach,
cucumber, spring onions
(scallions) and parsley in a bowl. Whisk
the oil, yogurt and wine vinegar until
well blended, and pour over the salad.

STEP 1

STEP 2

STEP 3

STEP 4

FISH & SEAFOOD CHOWDER

Served with warm crusty bread and a salad, this tasty soup makes a substantial lunch or supper dish.

SERVES 4

1 kg/2 lb mussels in their shells
1 large onion, thinly sliced
2 garlic cloves, chopped
3 bay leaves
a few stalks of parsley
a few stalks of thyme
300 ml/¹/₂ pint/1¹/₄ cups water
250 g/8 oz smoked haddock fillets
500 g/1 lb potatoes, peeled and diced
4 celery stalks, thickly sliced
1 x 250 g/8 oz can sweetcorn kernels, drained and rinsed
150 ml/¹/₄ pint/²/₃ cup natural yogurt
1 tsp cornflour (cornstarch)
150 ml/¹/₄ pint/²/₃ cup dry white wine, or dry cider
¹/₂ tsp cayenne pepper, or to taste
black pepper
2 tbsp chopped parsley

1 Scrub the mussels, pull off the "beards" and rinse in several changes of cold water. Discard any open shells that remain open when tapped.

2 Put the onion, garlic, bay leaves, parsley and thyme in a large pan and pour on the water. Add the mussels, cover and cook over high heat for 5 minutes, shaking the pan once or twice.

3 Line a colander with muslin or cheesecloth and stand it in a bowl. Strain the mussel liquor into the bowl. Remove and shell the mussels and set them aside. Discard the vegetables and herbs and reserve the liquor.

4 Put the haddock, potatoes and celery into the rinsed pan, add 600 ml/1 pint/2½ cups of cold water and bring to the boil. Cover the pan and simmer for 10 minutes. Remove the haddock with a fish slice and skin, bone and flake it. Remove the vegetables with a slotted spoon and strain the liquor into the reserved seafood liquor.

5 Return the cooking liquor to the rinsed pan, add the sweetcorn and bring to the boil. Stir together the yogurt and cornflour (cornstarch) to make a smooth paste. Stir in a little of the fish liquor, then pour it into the pan. Stir until the yogurt is well blended, then add the reserved mussels, haddock, potatoes and celery. Add the white wine, season with cayenne and black pepper and heat the soup gently, without boiling. Taste and adjust the seasoning if necessary. Transfer to a warm serving dish and sprinkle with the chopped parsley. Serve hot, with crusty bread.

SHRIMP CURRY & FRUIT SAUCE

Serve this lightly-spiced dish as part of a buffet meal, or as a refreshingly different lunch dish, with rice or poppadoms.

STEP 1

SERVES 4

2 tbsp vegetable oil
30 g/1 oz/2 tbsp butter
2 onions, finely chopped
2 garlic cloves, finely chopped
1 tsp cumin seeds, lightly crushed
1 tsp ground turmeric
1 tsp paprika
1/2 tsp chilli powder, or to taste
1/2 cucumber, thinly diced
60 g/2 oz creamed coconut
1 x 425 g/15 oz can chopped tomatoes
1 tbsp tomato purée (paste)
500 g/1 lb frozen shrimps, defrosted
150 ml/1/4 pint/2/3 cup Greek-style yogurt
2 hard-boiled eggs, quartered
salt
coriander and onion rings, to garnish

FRUIT SAUCE:

300 ml/1/2 pint/1 1/4 cups natural yogurt
1/4 tsp salt
1 garlic clove, crushed
2 tbsp chopped mint
4 tbsp seedless raisins
1 small pomegranate

1 Heat the oil and butter in a frying pan. Add the chopped onions and fry until translucent. Add the garlic and fry for a further minute, until softened but not browned.

2 Stir in the cumin seeds, turmeric, paprika and chilli powder and cook for 2 minutes, stirring. Stir in the creamed coconut, chopped tomatoes and tomato purée (paste) and bring to the boil. Simmer for 10 minutes, or until the sauce has thickened slightly. It should not be at all runny.

3 Remove the pan from the heat and set aside to cool. Stir in the shrimps, cucumber and yogurt. Taste the sauce and adjust the seasoning if necessary. Cover and chill until ready to serve.

4 To make the fruit sauce, place the yogurt in a bowl and stir in the salt, garlic, mint and raisins. Cut the pomegranate in half, scoop out the seeds and discard the white membrane. Stir the seeds into the yogurt, reserving a few for garnish.

5 Transfer the curry to a serving dish and arrange the hard-boiled egg, coriander and onion rings on top. Serve the sauce separately, sprinkled with the reserved pomegranate seeds.

STEP 2

STEP 3

STEP 4

CHAPTER THREE

Vegetables

Yogurt is the perfect low-fat partner in vegetable dishes
of all kinds, from Spinach Pancakes with an interesting
filling (page 32) to an elegant Cauliflower Roulade (page 28),
and gives vegetarian dishes a satisfyingly piquant taste.

Yogurt cheese proves its versatility in this chapter, too,
as a satisfying home-made substitute for either cottage
cheese or low-fat soft cheese. If you do decide to
extend your repertoire and try your hand at simple
cheesemaking, you will find tasty ways to
use it to delicious advantage. See page 52 for easy
instructions on how to make this tasty cheese.

Opposite: *The crisp fresh leaves
of vegetables and salads blend
perfectly with yogurt to make
healthy, low-fat dishes.*

STEP 3

STEP 4

STEP 6

STEP 7

CAULIFLOWER ROULADE

A light-as-air mixture of eggs and vegetables produces a stylish vegetarian dish that can be enjoyed hot or cold.

SERVES 6
OVEN: 200°C/400°F/GAS 6

1 small cauliflower, divided into florets
4 eggs, separated
90 g/ 3 oz/³/₄ cup Cheddar, grated
60 g/ 2 oz/¹/₄ cup yogurt cheese (see
   page 77), or cottage cheese
large pinch of grated nutmeg
¹/₂ tsp mustard powder
salt and pepper

FILLING:
1 bunch watercress, trimmed
60 g/ 2 oz/¹/₄ cup butter
30 g/ 1 oz/¹/₄ cup flour
175 ml/ 6 fl oz/³/₄ cup natural yogurt
30 g/ 1 oz/¹/₄ cup Cheddar, grated
60 g/ 2 oz/¹/₄ cup yogurt cheese (see
   page 77), or cottage cheese

1 Line a Swiss roll tin (pan) with baking parchment.

2 Steam the cauliflower until just tender. Drain and run cold water on it, to prevent further cooking. Place the cauliflower in a food processor and chop finely.

3 Beat the egg yolks, then stir in the cauliflower, 60 g/2 oz/½ cup of the

Cheddar and the yogurt cheese. Season with salt, nutmeg, mustard and pepper. Whisk the egg whites until stiff but not dry, then fold into the cauliflower mixture, using a metal spoon.

4 Spread the mixture evenly in the prepared tin (pan) and bake in the preheated oven for 20-25 minutes, until well risen and golden brown.

5 Finely chop the watercress, reserving a few sprigs for garnish. Melt the butter in a small pan and add the watercress. Cook for 3 minutes, stirring, until it has collapsed. Blend in the flour, then stir in the yogurt and simmer for 2 minutes. Stir in the cheeses.

6 Turn out the roulade on to a damp tea towel covered with baking parchment. Peel off the paper and leave 1 minute for the steam to escape. Roll up the roulade, including a new sheet of paper, starting from one narrow end.

7 Unroll the roulade, spread the filling to within 2.5 cm/1 in of the edges, and roll up tightly. Transfer to a baking sheet, sprinkle on the remaining Cheddar and return to the oven for 5 minutes. Serve hot or cold.

VEGETABLE MEDLEY

Serve this as a crisp and colourful vegetarian dish, with pitta bread, chapattis or naan, or as an accompaniment to roast or grilled meats.

STEP 1a

STEP 1b

STEP 3

SERVES 4

150 g/5 oz young, tender green beans
8 baby carrots
6 baby turnips
1/2 small cauliflower
2 tbsp vegetable oil
2 large onions, sliced
2 garlic cloves, finely chopped
300 ml/1/2 pint/1 1/4 cups natural yogurt
1 tbsp cornflour (cornstarch)
2 tbsp tomato purée (paste)
large pinch of chilli powder
salt

1 Top and tail the beans and snap them in half. Cut the carrots in half and the turnips in quarters. Divide the cauliflower into florets, discarding the thickest part of the stalk. Steam the vegetables over boiling, salted water for 3 minutes, then turn them into a colander and plunge them at once in a large bowl of cold water to prevent further cooking.

2 Heat the oil in a pan and fry the onions until they are translucent. Stir in the garlic and cook for 1 further minute.

3 Mix together the yogurt, cornflour (cornstarch) and tomato purée (paste) to form a smooth paste. Stir this paste into the onions in the pan and cook for 1-2 minutes until the sauce is well blended.

4 Drain the vegetables well, then gradually stir them into the sauce, taking care not to break them up. Season with salt and chilli powder to taste, cover and simmer gently for 5 minutes, until the vegetables are just tender. Taste and adjust the seasoning if necessary. Serve immediately.

PITTAS

You can serve this lightly-spiced vegetable dish as a filling for pitta pockets. To do this, thicken the sauce slightly by simmering it, uncovered, before adding the partly-cooked vegetables. To make the snack more substantial, you can serve the filled pittas with sizzling sausages or wooden skewers of grilled lamb.

STEP 4

STEP 1

STEP 3

STEP 4

STEP 5

SPINACH PANCAKES

Serve these pancakes as a light lunch or supper dish, with tomato and basil salad for a dramatic colour contrast.

SERVES 4
OVEN: 180°C/350°F/GAS 4

90 g/3 oz/³/₄ cup wholewheat flour
1 egg
150 ml/¹/₄ pint/²/₃ cup natural yogurt
3 tbsp water
1 tbsp vegetable oil, plus extra for brushing
200 g/7 oz frozen leaf spinach, defrosted and
    liquidized
pinch of grated nutmeg
salt and pepper
lemon wedges and coriander, to garnish

FILLING:
1 tbsp vegetable oil
3 spring onions (scallions), thinly sliced
250 g/8 oz/1 cup Ricotta
4 tbsp plain yogurt
90 g/3 oz/³/₄ cup Gruyère, grated
1 egg, lightly beaten
250 g/8 oz shelled prawns (shrimp), chopped
2 tbsp chopped parsley
pinch of cayenne pepper

1 Sift the flour and salt into a bowl and tip in any bran remaining in the sieve. Beat together the egg, yogurt, water and oil. Gradually pour it on to the flour, beating all the time. Stir in the spinach purée and season with pepper and nutmeg.

2 To make the filling, heat the oil in a pan and fry the onions until translucent. Remove with a slotted spoon and drain on paper towels. Beat together the Ricotta, yogurt and half the Gruyère. Beat in the egg and stir in the prawns (shrimp) and parsley. Season with salt and cayenne pepper.

3 Lightly brush a small, heavy frying pan with oil and heat. Pour in 3-4 tablespoons of the pancake batter and tilt the pan so that it covers the base. Cook for about 3 minutes, until bubbles appear in the centre. Turn and cook the other side for about 2 minutes, until lightly browned. Slide the pancake on a warmed plate, cover with foil and keep warm while you cook the remainder. It should make 8-12 pancakes.

4 Spread a little filling over each pancake and fold in half and then half again, envelope style. Spoon the remaining filling into the opening.

5 Grease a shallow, ovenproof dish and arrange the pancakes in a single layer. Sprinkle on the remaining cheese and cook in the preheated oven for about 15 minutes. Serve hot, garnished with lemon and coriander.

CHAPTER FOUR

Meat & Poultry

Leg of lamb coated with an aromatic paste of yogurt, herbs and spices; rabbit joints flavoured in a yogurt and herb marinade; tender cubes of lamb basted with yogurt and grilled until they are crisp on the outside, succulently pink inside; tandoori chicken baked in a spicy yogurt mixture which is served as a piquant sauce; moussaka baked until the yogurt and cheese custard topping is a sizzling toasty-brown – yogurt plays its part in meat dishes in so many ways.

Use it with olive oil, lemon juice, wine or vinegar in a marinade to tenderize the meat; use it in place of water or milk as a liquid element in pastry, and marvel at the difference it makes. And stir it into a sauce to complement meat meals from herb-flavoured meatballs to casseroled pork. These and other dishes show that yogurt is not just a tasty added ingredient. It has a practical part to play in the preparation of a wide range of classic and country-style dishes.

Opposite: An idyllic rural scene in Tuscany, producer of much splendid meat and game. Yogurt marinades, coatings and toppings combine perfectly with meat and poultry dishes of all kinds.

STEP 1

STEP 3

STEP 4

STEP 5

CRISPY-COATED POUSSINS

You could adapt this recipe using a whole chicken or chicken pieces,
serving them on the bed of moist and colourful vegetables.

SERVES 6
OVEN: 180°C/350°F/GAS 4

4 tbsp vegetable oil
60 g/2 oz/¹/₄ cup butter
6 small poussins, trussed
1 large onion, sliced
500 g/1 lb baby carrots
1 tbsp flour
150 ml/¹/₄ pint/²/₃ cup white wine
juice of 2 oranges
2 fennel bulbs, quartered
300 ml/¹/₂ pint/1¹/₄ cups chicken stock
1 tbsp green peppercorns, lightly crushed
¹/₂ tsp salt
1 tsp cornflour (cornstarch)
150 ml/¹/₄ pint/²/₃ cup Greek-style yogurt

COATING:
3 tbsp demerara sugar
1 tbsp green peppercorns, lightly crushed
3 tbsp coarse sea salt
150 ml/¹/₄ pint/²/₃ cup Greek-style yogurt

1 Heat the oil in a large frying pan and add the butter. When bubbling, add the poussins in batches and brown evenly on all sides. Remove and keep warm.

2 Add the onion to the pan and fry until translucent. Add the carrots , stir to coat evenly, then sprinkle on the flour and blend well. Pour on the wine and orange juice, stirring all the time. Add the fennel, chicken stock and peppercorns and season. Bring to the boil then pour into a large roasting pan.

3 Arrange the poussins in the roasting pan, cover loosely with foil and cook in the preheated oven for 40 minutes.

4 To make the coating, stir together the sugar, peppercorns, salt and yogurt to make a thick paste.

5 Preheat the grill (broiler) to high. Remove the poussins from the roasting tin and place them on a rack. Spread the paste evenly over the poussins then grill (broil) for 3-4 minutes, until the coating is crisp.

6 Arrange the drained vegetables on a warm serving dish. Place the roasting tin over medium heat and bring the sauce to the boil. Stir the cornflour (cornstarch) into the yogurt then blend into the sauce. Taste for seasoning. Place the poussins in the centre of the dish, spoon a little sauce over the vegetables, and serve the rest separately.

STEP 2

STEP 3

STEP 4

STEP 5

LAMB KEBABS & CUCUMBER SAUCE

*Serve the kebabs sizzling hot and the sauce as cool as can be –
it is a delicious partnership.*

SERVES 4

1 kg/ 2 lb lean leg of lamb, trimmed of fat
3 tbsp olive oil
1 tbsp red wine vinegar
juice of ½ lemon
3 tbsp natural yogurt
1 tbsp dried oregano
2 large garlic cloves, crushed
2 dried bay leaves, crumbled
4 fresh bay leaves
2 tbsp chopped parsley
salt and pepper

SAUCE:
300 ml/ ½ pint/ 1 ¼ cups natural yogurt
1 garlic clove, crushed
¼ tsp salt
½ small cucumber, peeled and finely chopped
3 tbsp finely chopped mint
pinch of paprika

1 Cut the lamb into cubes about 4-5 cm/1½-2 in square. Pat dry with paper towels. This will help to ensure that the meat is crisp and firm on the outside when grilled (broiled).

2 Whisk together the olive oil, wine vinegar, lemon juice and yogurt. Stir in the oregano, garlic and crumbled bay leaves and season.

3 Place the meat cubes in the marinade and stir until well coated in the mixture. Cover and place in the refrigerator for at least 2 hours, for the meat to absorb the flavours.

4 Meanwhile, make the sauce. Place the yogurt in a large bowl. Stir in the garlic, salt, cucumber and mint. Cover and set aside in the refrigerator. If it is more convenient, the sauce may be made several hours in advance.

5 Heat the grill (broiler) to high. With a slotted spoon, lift the meat from the marinade and shake off any excess liquid. Divide the meat into 4 equal portions. Thread the meat and the fresh bay leaves on to 4 skewers.

6 Grill (broil) the kebabs for about 4 minutes on each side, basting frequently with the marinade. At this stage the meat should be crisp on the outside and slightly pink on the inside. If you prefer it well done, cook the kebabs for a little longer.

7 Sprinkle the kebabs with parsley and serve at once with a tomato salad. Sprinkle the paprika over the sauce and serve chilled.

STEP 1

STEP 2

STEP 5

STEP 6

MOUSSAKA

*Both the meat sauce and the custard topping are lightly flavoured
with cumin for a truly Greek flavour.*

SERVES 6
OVEN: 190°C/375°F/GAS 5

750 g/1¹/₂ lb aubergines (eggplant), thinly
  sliced
6 tbsp olive oil, plus extra for brushing
2 large onions, finely chopped
2 large garlic cloves, finely chopped
750 g/1¹/₂ lb lean lamb, minced
2 tbsp tomato purée (paste)
¹/₂ tsp ground cumin
salt and pepper
5 tbsp chopped coriander, or parsley

TOPPING:
4 eggs
600 ml/1 pint/2¹/₂ cups natural yogurt
¹/₂ tsp ground cumin
60 g/2 oz/¹/₄ cup feta cheese, crumbled
pepper
30 g/1 oz/¹/₄ cup Gruyère, grated

1 Put the aubergines (eggplant) in a
colander over a bowl and sprinkle
with salt. Leave for about 1 hour, while
the salt draws out the bitter juices, then
rinse under cold, running water. Drain
and pat dry with paper towels.

2 Heat 2 tablespoons of the oil in a
frying pan. Fry half the aubergine
(eggplant) slices, turning them once,
until evenly brown on both sides.
Remove and keep warm. Heat another 2
tablespoons of the oil and fry the
remaining slices in the same way.
Remove and keep warm.

3 Add the remaining oil to the pan
and fry the onions until they are a
light, golden brown. Stir in the chopped
garlic. Add the meat to the pan and fry,
stirring, until it changes colour.

4 Stir in the tomato purée (paste)
and cumin and season. Remove
the pan from the heat and stir in the
coriander or parsley.

5 Brush a large ovenproof dish with
olive oil. Arrange half the
aubergine (eggplant) slices in the dish.
Cover with the meat mixture, then
arrange the remaining aubergine
(eggplant) on top.

6 To make the topping, beat the
eggs, then beat in the yogurt. Add
the cumin and feta cheese, and season
with pepper. Pour the sauce over the
dish, and sprinkle on the grated cheese.
Bake in the preheated oven for 45-50
minutes, until the top is dark golden
brown and bubbling. Serve hot.

STEP 2

STEP 3

STEP 4

STEP 5

ORCHARD PORK

This is a quick and easy dish, ideal to serve to unexpected guests.

SERVES 4

60 g/ 2 oz/¹/₄ cup butter
1 onion, chopped
1 garlic clove, finely chopped
500 g/ 1 lb pork tenderloin (fillet)
1 tbsp paprika
150 ml/¹/₄ pint/²/₃ cup chicken stock
300 ml/¹/₂ pint/ 1¹/₄ cups natural yogurt
2 tsp cornflour (cornstarch)
2 dessert apples
juice of ¹/₂ lemon
salt and pepper
parsley sprigs, to garnish
sautéd baby vegetables, to garnish (optional)

1 Heat half the butter in a frying pan over a medium heat. Fry the onion until it is translucent. Then stir in the garlic and fry for 1 minute more.

2 Trim the pork of excess fat and cut into small thin slices. Pat the meat dry with paper towels. Add the pork to the pan, sprinkle on the paprika and stir until the meat is coated with the spice. Cook for 3 minutes, stirring once or twice.

3 Pour in the chicken stock and stir well. Bring to the boil, cover the pan and simmer for 10 minutes.

4 Mix together the yogurt and cornflour (cornstarch) to make a smooth, thin paste. Stir it into the pork, season and continue cooking for 10 minutes, stirring occasionally. Do not overheat or it will curdle.

5 Heat the remaining butter in a frying pan. Core and slice the apples and fry until they are golden brown on both sides.

6 Stir the lemon juice into the sauce and taste to check the seasoning. Transfer the meat to a warmed serving dish, arrange the apple slices on top and garnish with parsley. Serve with baby vegetables, if liked.

MICROWAVE METHOD

Place half the butter in a dish and cook on high for 3 minutes. Stir in the pork and paprika, cover and cook on high for 6 minutes. Add the stock, cover and cook on high for 5 minutes. Stir in the yogurt, cornflour (cornstarch) and seasoning, cover and cook on high for 4 minutes, stirring once. Remove the dish, stir, cover again and stand for 5 minutes. Heat the remaining butter in a separate dish on high for 1 minute. Add the apples and cook on high for 3 minutes, stirring once.

STEP 1

STEP 2

STEP 4

STEP 5

HAM & CHICKEN PIE

Made with yogurt shortcrust pastry, this pie has a really melt-in-the-mouth crust and a moist filling.

SERVES 6
OVEN: 200°C/400°F/GAS 6

250 g/8 oz/2 cups flour, plus extra for
    dusting
¹/₂ tsp mustard powder
¹/₄ tsp salt
175 g/6 oz/³/₄ cup butter, cut into small
    pieces, plus extra for greasing
about 3 tbsp natural yogurt
2 tbsp milk
dill sprigs, to garnish

FILLING:
60 g/2 oz/¹/₄ cup butter
30 g/1 oz/¹/₄ cup flour
150 ml/¹/₄ pint/²/₃ cup milk
150 ml/¹/₄ pint/²/₃ cup natural yogurt
2 small leeks, sliced
250g/8 oz boned, skinned chicken breast,
    diced
250 g (8 oz) diced ham
1 tsp mushroom ketchup, or soy sauce
black pepper

1 Grease a loose-bottomed flan tin,
4 cm/1¾ in deep. Sift together the
flour, mustard powder and salt and rub
in the butter until the mixture resembles
fine breadcrumbs. Stir in just enough
yogurt to make a firm and non-sticky
dough. Wrap in foil and chill.

2 Melt 30 g/1 oz/2 tbsp of the butter
in a small pan over a medium heat.
Blend in the flour then pour on the milk
and yogurt, stirring all the time. Simmer,
uncovered, for 5 minutes, then remove
from the heat, transfer the sauce to a
bowl and leave to cool.

3 Melt the remaining butter in a
small pan and fry the leeks for 2-3
minutes, until they begin to soften.

4 Stir the leeks into the white sauce,
add the chicken and ham, and
cook for 3 minutes, until the chicken has
changed colour. Add the ketchup or soy
sauce, and season, then leave to cool
completely.

5 Roll out the pastry on a lightly-
floured board. Use just over half of
it to line the prepared tin. Pour in the
cold filling. Roll out the remaining
pastry and cover the pie. Trim the edges
and press them together. Brush the top
with milk. Re-roll the pastry trimmings
and cut into decorative shapes such as
leaves or stars. Arrange the shapes over
the pie and brush with milk. Bake the pie
in the preheated oven for 35 minutes, or
until the pastry is golden brown. Serve
hot or cold.

TANDOORI CHICKEN

The yogurt and spices used to marinate the dish are served as a piquant sauce which may be poured over plain, boiled rice.

STEP 2

STEP 3a

STEP 3b

STEP 5

SERVES 4

OVEN: 200°C/400°F/GAS 6

150 ml/¼ pint/⅔ cup natural yogurt
½ tsp salt
1 tsp ground turmeric
1 tsp cumin seeds
1 tsp ground ginger
1 tsp garam masala
1 tsp chilli powder, or to taste
3 garlic cloves, crushed
4 bay leaves, crumbled
2 tbsp tomato purée (paste)
juice of 2 limes, or 1 lemon
4 portions of chicken, about 350 g/12 oz
    each, skinned
125 g/4 oz/½ cup Clarified Butter (see
    page 78)
2 tbsp paprika
Spiced Courgettes (Zucchini), to serve (see
    page 78)

1 Put the yogurt in a bowl and stir in the salt, turmeric, cumin seeds, ginger, garam masala and chilli powder. Stir until well blended, then stir in the garlic, bay leaves, tomato purée (paste) and lime or lemon juice.

2 Pour half the yogurt marinade into a shallow dish, spread evenly over the base and place the chicken pieces in a single layer on top. Spoon the remaining marinade over the chicken pieces to cover them completely. Loosely cover with foil and chill for at least 3 hours, or overnight. Spoon the marinade over the chicken from time to time.

3 Line a roasting tin with a piece of foil large enough to enclose it. Remove the chicken from the marinade and allow any excess to drain back into the bowl. Place the chicken pieces in the tin in a single layer. Pour the clarified butter over the chicken. Fold the foil over the tin and seal the edges so that no steam can escape.

4 Cook the chicken for 1 hour, then open the foil. Sprinkle the chicken evenly with paprika and return to the oven, uncovered, for a further 15 minutes.

5 Make the Spiced Courgettes (Zucchini) (see page 78).

6 Transfer the chicken to a warmed serving dish with the Spiced Courgettes (Zucchini). Strain the marinade into a small pan, bring to the boil and boil rapidly for 2-3 minutes to reduce. Serve separately.

STEP 2

STEP 3

STEP 4

STEP 5

SPICY MEATBALLS

The creamy sauce is an ideal contrast to the spiciness of the meatballs, and an unusual way of presenting beef.

𝄢

SERVES 4

4 tbsp olive oil
1 large onion, finely chopped
2 garlic cloves, finely chopped
500 g/ 1 lb lean minced beef
90 g/ 3 oz/ ¾ cup dry breadcrumbs
2 tbsp chopped coriander or parsley
1 tsp cayenne pepper
3 tbsp natural yogurt
juice of ½ lemon
salt and pepper
flour, for dusting
30 g/ 1 oz/ 2 tbsp butter
noodles, to serve

SAUCE:
1 tbsp plain flour
175 ml/ 6 fl oz/ ¾ cup chicken stock
150 g/ ¼ pint/ ⅔ cup natural yogurt
1 tbsp chopped coriander

1 Heat 2 tablespoons of the oil in a frying pan and fry the onion until it is transparent. Add the garlic, and fry for 1 minute more. Set aside to cool.

2 Put the meat in a bowl and mash with a wooden spoon until it forms a sticky paste. Add the onion mixture, breadcrumbs and coriander or parsley. Stir in the paprika and cayenne pepper

and mix well. Stir in the yogurt and lemon juice, season and stir until it forms a thick, sticky paste. Cover and chill for at least 30 minutes.

3 Flour your hands and shape the mixture into rounds about the size of table-tennis balls. Roll each one in flour until evenly coated.

4 Heat the remaining oil and the butter in the frying pan and fry the meatballs for 7-8 minutes, until they are firm, and lightly coloured on all sides. Remove with a slotted spoon.

5 To make the sauce, stir the flour into the remaining oil and fat. When well blended, gradually pour on the chicken stock, stirring constantly. Season and bring to the boil. Add the meatballs, cover and simmer over low heat for 30 minutes, turning the meatballs once or twice.

6 Stir in the yogurt, and taste for seasoning. Slowly reheat without bringing it to the boil. Remove from the heat and stir in half the coriander. Transfer to a serving dish and sprinkle with remaining coriander. Serve with buttered noodles.

ROAST LEG OF LAMB

Prepare the lamb at least a day in advance and leave it in the refrigerator so that the flavours can permeate the meat.

STEP 1

STEP 3

STEP 5

STEP 6

SERVES 6
OVEN: 220°C/425°F/GAS 7;
THEN 180°C/350°F/GAS 4

1 x 50 g/1½ oz can anchovies, drained
1.8 kg/4 lb leg of lamb
2 tbsp coriander seeds
4 large garlic cloves, crushed
300 ml/½ pint/1¼ cups natural yogurt
6-8 tbsp chopped parsley
1 bottle dry white wine
juice of 1 lemon
500 g/1 lb small button onions, peeled and
    left whole
45 g/1½ oz/3 tbsp butter
30 g/1 oz/2 tbsp caster sugar
150 ml/¼ pint/⅔ cup water
salt and pepper
fresh herbs, to garnish
new potatoes tossed in butter and parsley, to
    serve

1 Cut the anchovies in half and split them lengthways. Using a small, sharp knife make slits all over the lamb and insert the anchovy pieces, folding if necessary to push them in.

2 Lightly crush the coriander seeds in a pestle and mortar. Tip them into a bowl, stir in the garlic, yogurt and parsley and season with pepper.

3 Spread the yogurt paste evenly over the lamb, using the back of a spoon to press it into the meat. Place the lamb in a shallow dish, cover loosely with foil and leave in the refrigerator for 1-2 days, turning it once or twice.

4 Transfer the lamb to a roasting pan. Pour in the wine and lemon juice and cook uncovered for 15 minutes. Lower the heat and continue roasting for a further 1-1¼ hours, basting frequently.

5 Remove the meat from the oven, cover with foil and leave to rest in a warm place for at least 15 minutes. Pour the juices into a small pan and boil rapidly to reduce. Taste for seasoning.

6 Blanch the onions in boiling, salted water for 3 minutes, then drain and dry on paper towels. Melt the butter in a pan and add the onions, sugar and water. Simmer, uncovered, for 15 minutes, turning frequently. Watch carefully towards the end, as the water evaporates and the sugar caramelizes.

7 Transfer the meat to a serving dish and spoon the onions around. Serve with new potatoes and serve the sauce separately.

STEP 2

STEP 3a

STEP 3b

STEP 4

RABBIT WITH FRIED CHEESE

*The topping is a simple but exquisite refinement to a country dish
of casseroled rabbit.*

SERVES 4
OVEN: 170°C/325°F/GAS 3

*1 kg/2 lb rabbit joints, washed and dried
salt
1 tbsp vegetable oil
45 g/1¹/₂ oz/3 tbsp butter
45 g/1¹/₂ oz/6 tbsp flour
300 ml/¹/₂ pint/1¹/₄ cups chicken stock
2 tsp Dijon mustard
freshly ground black pepper
4 tbsp plain yogurt*

MARINADE:
*2 tbsp olive oil
1 small onion, sliced
150 ml/¹/₄ pint/²/₃ cup dry cider
2 tbsp white wine vinegar
2 sprigs each of rosemary and thyme
¹/₂ tsp juniper berries, crushed
¹/₂ tsp coriander seeds, crushed
150 ml/¹/₄ pint/²/₃ cup natural yogurt*

TOPPING:
*250g/8 oz/1 cup yogurt cheese (see
    page 77), cut into 4 slices
2 tbsp flour seasoned with 1 tsp dried thyme
    and freshly-ground black pepper
3 tbsp olive oil*

1 Put all the marinade ingredients
except the yogurt in a small pan.

Bring to the boil, remove from the heat
and allow to cool completely.

2 Beat the yogurt into the cold
marinade, and pour into a shallow
dish. Put the rabbit in the dish and spoon
over the marinade. Cover and chill for
several hours.

3 Heat the oil and butter in a
casserole. Drain the rabbit then fry
until golden brown. Remove with a
slotted spoon and stir in the flour. Pour
the marinade into the casserole and
blend. Stir in the stock and mustard, and
season.

4 Return the rabbit to the casserole,
bring to the boil and cover. Cook in
the preheated oven for 1-1½ hours until
tender – test with a skewer. Strain the
sauce into a pan, stir in the yogurt and
check the seasoning. Pour the sauce over
the rabbit.

5 To make the topping, toss the
yogurt cheese in the seasoned
flour. Heat the oil in a frying pan and fry
the cheese for 2 minutes on each side,
until golden brown. Place the cheese on
the rabbit and serve, garnished with
rosemary.

CHAPTER FIVE

Desserts & Cakes

Yogurt's credentials as a tasty and delicious substitute for cream are never more convincing than in desserts and baked goods. By using cream and yogurt in equal proportions in crème brûlée, for example, you can retain the full dairy flavour with a significant reduction in fat and calorie content. By using yogurt in place of milk in a batter mixture you can introduce a surprising tanginess that contrasts well with the sweetness of fruit or an accompanying sauce, and by substituting plain yogurt for double (heavy) cream in a luxurious cheesecake mixture you can serve a dinner party dessert that some guests might otherwise have considered over-rich.

Yogurt can be used to practical advantage, too, in traditional baking. Use it in place of buttermilk in light-as-a-feather sweet or savoury scones and in traditional gingerbread where its blandness perfectly complements the rich combination of black treacle, dark brown sugar and dried fruits.

Opposite: *Guilt-free enjoyment of rich desserts is now possible, thanks to tangy, low-fat yogurt.*

STEP 2a

STEP 2b

STEP 3

STEP 4

APRICOT BRULEE

Serve this delicious dessert with caramelized meringues (see recipe below) for an extra-special occasion.

SERVES 6

125 g/4 oz/²/₃ cup unsulphured apricots
150 ml/¹/₄ pint/²/₃ cup orange juice
4 egg yolks
2 tbsp caster sugar
150 ml/¹/₄ pint/²/₃ cup yogurt
150 ml/¹/₄ pint/²/₃ cup double (heavy)
* cream*
1 tsp vanilla flavouring
90 g/3 oz/¹/₂ cup demerara sugar
caramelized meringues to serve, optional

1 Place the apricots and orange juice in a bowl and soak for at least 1 hour. Pour into a small pan, bring slowly to the boil and simmer for 20 minutes. Purée in a blender or food processor.

2 Beat together the egg yolks and sugar until the mixture is light and fluffy. Place the yogurt in a small pan, add the vanilla and bring to the boil over a low heat. Pour the yogurt mixture over the eggs, beating all the time, then transfer to the top of a double boiler, or place the bowl over a pan of simmering water. Stir until the custard thickens.

3 Place the apricot mixture in 6 ramekins and carefully pour on the custard. Cool, then leave to chill.

4 Heat the grill (broiler) to high. Sprinkle the demerara sugar evenly over the custard and grill (broil) until the sugar caramelizes. Set aside to cool. To serve the brûlée, crack the hard caramel topping with the back of a tablespoon.

CARAMELIZED MERINGUES:
4 egg whites
90 g/3 oz/6 tbsp caster sugar
60 g/2 oz/4 tbsp granulated sugar
30 g/1 oz/¹/₄ cup blanched almonds, toasted

Whisk the egg whites until stiff. Whisk in the caster sugar a little at a time, then whisk until the mixture is glossy and forms peaks. Pour water into a shallow frying pan until 1 cm/½ in deep and bring to simmering point. Take scoops of meringue, using 2 tablespoons, and place in the gently simmering water. Poach for 2 minutes, turning them over once: do not allow the water to boil. Remove with a slotted spoon and place on baking parchment. For the caramel, place the granulated sugar in a small, heavy pan over a low heat. Shake the pan to distribute the sugar evenly, then leave it to caramelize, without stirring. Do not leave the pan unattended. Transfer the meringues to a serving dish, pour on the caramel and scatter the almonds on top.

STEP 1

STEP 2

STEP 4

STEP 5

CHOCOLATE CHIP ICE-CREAM

This frozen dessert offers the best of both worlds, delicious cookies and a rich dairy-flavoured ice.

SERVES 6

300 ml/¹/₂ pint/ 1¹/₄ cups milk
1 vanilla pod
2 eggs
2 egg yolks
60 g/ 2 oz/¹/₄ cup caster sugar
300 ml/¹/₂ pint/ 1¹/₄ cups natural yogurt
125 g/ 4 oz Chocolate Chip Cookies, broken
  into small pieces (see page 77).

1 Pour the milk into a small pan, add the vanilla pod and bring slowly to the boil. Remove from the heat, cover the pan and leave to cool.

2 Beat the eggs and egg yolks in a double boiler, or in a bowl over a pan of simmering water. Add the sugar and continue beating until the mixture is pale and creamy.

3 Reheat the milk to simmering point and strain it over the egg mixture. Stir continuously until the custard is thick enough to coat the back of a spoon. Remove the custard from the heat and stand the pan or bowl in cold water to prevent any further cooking. Wash and dry the vanilla pod for future use. (See right for advice on using and storing vanilla pods.)

4 Stir the yogurt into the cooled custard and beat until it is well blended. When the mixture is thoroughly cold, stir in the broken cookies.

5 Transfer the mixture to a chilled metal cake tin or polythene container, cover and freeze for 4 hours. Remove from the freezer every hour, transfer to a chilled bowl and beat vigorously, to prevent ice crystals forming. Alternatively, freeze the mixture in an ice-cream maker, following the manufacturer's instructions.

6 To serve the ice-cream, transfer it to the main part of the refrigerator for 1 hour. Serve in scoops.

VANILLA PODS

Vanilla pods can be used to flavour any hot liquid. For a stronger flavour, split the pod lengthwise with a sharp knife before infusing it in the hot liquid for 20-30 minutes. For a very strong flavour, scrape the seeds out of the pod and add to the liquid when infusing. Rinse and dry the pod after use. It can be stored in a jar of sugar, to impart its flavour.

PASHKA

A Russian dessert traditionally served at Easter, this dish is begun at least 24 hours before serving.

SERVES 8

900 ml/ 1½ pints/ 3½ cups natural yogurt
2 eggs
125 g/ 4 oz/ ½ cup golden caster sugar
150 g/ 5 oz/ ⅔ cup unsalted butter, softened
150 ml/ ¼ pint/ ⅔ cup double (heavy)
   cream
60 g/ 2 oz/ ⅓ cup candied orange peel,
   chopped
60 g/ 2 oz/ ⅓ cup dried apricots, chopped
90 g/ 3 oz/ ½ cup seedless raisins
90 g/ 3oz/ ¾ cup blanched almonds, chopped
1 tsp orange-flower water

TO DECORATE:

A selection of candied stalks and fruits, such
   as angelica, pineapple, greengages, pears
   and glacé cherries

1 Begin by making the yogurt cheese. Tip the yogurt into a colander lined with muslin or cheesecloth. Draw up the ends, tie firmly and hang up the bag to drain overnight.

2 Turn the drained yogurt cheese into a large bowl. Beat together the eggs and sugar until they are light and fluffy, then gradually beat the mixture into the yogurt cheese. Beat in the butter, then stir in the double (heavy) cream.

3 Stir the candied peel, apricots, raisins and almonds into the cheese mixture, then sprinkle on the orange-flower water and stir it in.

4 Thoroughly wash and dry a flower pot and line it with 2 layers of muslin or cheesecloth. Spoon the mixture into the pot and fold over the ends of the cloth to enclose it. Stand the pot in a dish and place a small plate on top so that it fits just inside the rim. Place a heavy weight or some food cans on top and place the pot in the refrigerator for at least 12 hours.

5 To turn out the dessert, unfold the cheesecloth, place a serving dish over the top of the container and invert it. When the dessert has been released, carefully ease away the cloth.

6 Decorate the top and sides of the dessert with slices of candied fruits arranged in a pattern. The bright green angelica can be used to represent leaves or stalks. Serve the dessert chilled, cut into wedge-shaped slices.

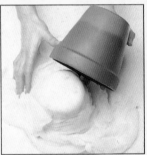

STEP 2

STEP 3

STEP 5a

STEP 5b

BOSTON CHOCOLATE PIE

*A lighter version of the popular chocolate cream pie,
this dessert is made with yogurt pastry.*

SERVES 6
OVEN: 200°C/400°F/GAS 6.

*250 g/8 oz Yogurt Shortcrust Pastry (see
page 44), but omit the mustard powder*

FILLING:
*3 eggs
125 g/4 oz/¹/₂ cup caster sugar
60 g/2 oz/¹/₂ cup flour, plus extra for
dusting
1 tbsp icing (confectioner's) sugar
pinch of salt
1 tsp vanilla flavouring
400 ml/14 fl oz/1¹/₄ cups milk
150 ml/¹/₄ pint/²/₃ cup natural yogurt
150 g/5 oz plain chocolate, broken into
pieces
2 tbsp kirsch*

TOPPING:
*150 ml/¹/₄ pint/²/₃ cup crème fraîche
Chocolate Caraque (see page 77)*

1 Grease a 23 cm/9 in loose-bottomed flan tin. Roll out the pastry on a lightly-floured board and lower into the flan ring. Press into the ring and around the sides and roll the rolling pin over the top to trim it neatly. Prick the base with a fork, line with baking parchment and fill it with dried beans. Bake "blind" for 20 minutes, then remove the beans and paper and return to the oven for 5 minutes to dry. Remove from the oven and leave on a wire rack to cool.

2 To make the filling, beat the eggs and sugar until light and fluffy. Put the flour, icing (confectioner's) sugar and salt in a sieve, sift over the beaten eggs and stir until thoroughly blended. Stir in the vanilla flavouring.

3 Put the milk and yogurt in a small pan, bring slowly to the boil, then strain on to the egg mixture. Pour into the top of a double boiler, or a bowl over a pan of simmering water, and stir until thick enough to coat the back of a spoon.

4 Put the chocolate and kirsch into a small pan over a low heat. When it has melted, stir into the custard. Remove the custard from the heat and stand the double boiler or bowl in cold water to prevent further cooking. Leave it to cool.

5 Make the Chocolate Caraque (see page 77). Pour the chocolate mixture into the pastry case. Spread the crème fraîche over the chocolate, and arrange the caraque rolls on top.

62

STEP 1

STEP 2

STEP 3

STEP 4

CHERRY CLAFOUTIS

A sweet batter pudding that has its origins in both England and France; it may be eaten straight from the oven, or slightly warm.

SERVES 4-6
OVEN:190°C/375°F/GAS 5

3 eggs
3 tbsp flour
pinch of salt
¹/₂ tbsp ground cinnamon
4 tbsp caster sugar, plus extra for sprinkling
300 ml/¹/₂ pint/ 1¹/₄ cups milk
150 ml/¹/₄ pint/²/₃ cup natural yogurt
2 tbsp dark rum (optional)
750 g/ 1¹/₂ lb black cherries, stalks removed, and pitted
15 g/¹/₂ oz/ 1 tbsp butter, plus extra for greasing

1 Grease a shallow, ovenproof dish. Lightly beat the eggs in a bowl. Put the flour, salt and cinnamon in a sieve, sift the dry ingredients over the eggs and beat the mixture until it is pale and creamy.

2 Pour the milk, yogurt and rum into a small pan and heat to simmering point. Pour over the egg mixture and beat thoroughly.

3 Place the cherries in the base of the prepared dish and spoon the batter over them. Dot the butter over the top of the pudding.

4 Bake the pudding in the preheated oven for 30 minutes, or until it is well risen and golden brown on top. To test, insert a fine skewer into the centre: it should come out clean. Sprinkle the pudding with caster sugar, and serve hot or warm.

VARIATION

Clafoutis limousin is a traditional French batter pudding (they leave the stones in the cherries). Make in the same way, let cool until just warm – it will sink slightly – then sprinkle with 2-3 tablespoons of Armagnac and a little icing (confectioner's) sugar.

STEP 1

STEP 2

STEP 3

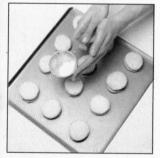

STEP 4

YOGURT SCONES

Yogurt is a suitable alternative to buttermilk, providing just the acidity needed to produce perfect scones. This basic recipe can be varied in many ways.

Makes about 16 Scones
Oven: 230°C/450°F/Gas 8

250 g/8 oz/2 cups flour, plus extra for
    dusting
1 tsp salt
1 tbsp baking powder
60 g/2 oz/¹/₄ cup unsalted butter, chilled,
    plus extra for greasing
60 g/2 oz/¹/₄ cup sugar
1 egg
6 tbsp natural yogurt

1 Sift together the flour, salt and baking powder. Cut the butter into small pieces, and rub it into the dry ingredients until the mixture resembles dry breadcrumbs. Stir in the sugar.

2 Beat together the egg and yogurt and stir it quickly into the dry ingredients. Mix to form a thick dough and knead until it is smooth and free from cracks.

3 Lightly flour a pastry board or work top and rolling pin and roll out the dough to a thickness of 1.5 cm/¾ in. Cut out rounds with a 5 cm/2 in pastry cutter, gather up the trimmings and roll them out again. Cut out as many more rounds as possible.

4 Grease a baking sheet lightly with butter and heat it in the oven. Transfer the dough rounds to the sheet and dust lightly with flour.

5 Bake the scones in the oven for 10 minutes, or until they are well risen and golden brown. Transfer them to a wire rack to cool. Serve the scones warm, with honey, jam or fruit jelly and with butter and whipped cream.

VARIATIONS

You can vary the recipe to make a selection of sweet and savoury scones:
For spiced scones, sift up to 1½ teaspoons ground ginger or cinnamon with the flour and other dry ingredients.
For dried fruit, seed or nut scones, stir in up to 60 g/2 oz/½ cup sultanas, currants, chopped dried apricots, dates or figs; up to 2 tablespoons sunflower seeds, or up to 60 g/2 oz/½ cup chopped walnuts, hazelnuts, almonds or pecans. These ingredients should be stirred in with the sugar at the end of step 1.
For savoury scones, omit the sugar in the recipe. At the end of step 1, stir in up to 45g/1½ oz/⅓ cup grated Cheddar or other hard cheese; up to 2 teaspoons dried herbs such as organo or thyme or up to 5 teaspoons fresh chopped herbs.

make custard for TRIFLE

TRY 3 egg yolks 1 tbl.
Sugar 1 tea cornflour
Vanilla

½ pint D Cream

STEP 1

STEP 3a

STEP 3b

STEP 5

TRUFFLE CHEESECAKE

The combination of flavours that are built up through the layers, from almond through coffee to chocolate, make this dessert a memorable experience.

SERVES 8
OVEN: 200°C/400°F/GAS 6;
THEN 140°C/275°F/GAS 1

60 g/2oz/¼ cup unsalted butter
125 g/4oz Amaretti biscuits, crushed
250 g/8 oz/1 cup yogurt cheese (see page 77) or low-fat soft cheese
250 g/8 oz/1 cup Mascarpone
150 ml/¼ pint/⅔ cup crème fraîche
½ tsp vanilla flavouring
90 g/3 oz/6 tbsp golden caster sugar
2 eggs, plus 1 egg yolk
1 tbsp flour
1 tbsp instant coffee granules
125 ml/4 fl oz/½ cup boiling water
2 tbsp coffee liqueur, or brandy
7 sponge finger (boudoir) biscuits

TOPPING:
15 g/½ oz/1 tbsp unsalted butter
150 ml/¼ pint/⅔ cup natural yogurt
60 g/2oz/¼ cup golden caster sugar
125 g/4 oz plain chocolate, broken up
1 tbsp coffee liqueur or brandy
1 tbsp cocoa powder

1 Grease and line a 18 cm/7 in loose-bottomed cake tin (pan). Melt the butter in a small pan over low heat. Remove from the heat, stir in the crumbs and tip them into the prepared tin (pan).

Press the crumbs to cover the base evenly and chill.

2 Beat together the yogurt cheese, mascarpone, crème fraîche and vanilla. Beat in the sugar, eggs, egg yolk and flour. Pour half into the tin (pan).

3 Dissolve the coffee in the boiling water, add the liqueur and pour into a small bowl. Quickly dip the sponge biscuits in the coffee. Arrange the biscuits over the cheese mixture and spoon on the remainder.

4 Bake in the preheated oven for 20 minutes, then lower the heat and cook for a further 1½ hours, or until a fine skewer inserted in the centre comes out clean. Allow the cake to cool completely before removing it from the tin (pan).

5 Bring the butter, yogurt and sugar to the boil. Add the chocolate and liqueur and stir over a low heat for 2-3 minutes. Remove from the heat and beat to blend thoroughly. Leave until completely cold, then spoon the mixture into a piping bag and pipe lines or squiggles over the top of the cheesecake. Just before serving, dust the top with cocoa powder.

DANISH LEMON CAKE

Cardamom seeds, the familiar flavouring of Danish pastries, contribute a subtle spiciness to this light sandwich cake.

SERVES 6-8
OVEN: 190°C/375°F/GAS 5

175 g/6 oz/¾ cup butter or margarine,
  softened, plus extra for greasing
175 g/6 oz/¾ cup golden caster sugar
3 eggs
175 g/6 oz/1½ cups self-raising flour,
  sifted, plus extra for dusting
2 tsp grated lemon rind
1 tbsp lemon juice
2 tbsp natural yogurt
8 cardamom pods

FILLING:
4 tbsp natural yogurt
4 tbsp icing (confectioner's) sugar, sifted,
  plus extra for dusting
4 tbsp lemon curd

1 Grease 2 x 18 cm/7 in diameter
  sponge sandwich tins (pans) and
dust them with flour. In a bowl beat
together the butter or margarine and
the sugar until the mixture is pale and
golden. Beat in the eggs one at a time,
beating in a tablespoon of the sifted
flour after each addition to prevent the
mixture from curdling. Fold in the
remaining flour with a metal spoon,
then stir in the lemon rind, lemon juice
and yogurt.

2 Split the cardamom pods with a
  small, sharp knife. Remove the
hard, black seeds and crush them with a
pestle and mortar, or tap them lightly
with a small hammer. Discard the pods
and stir the crushed seeds into the cake
mixture.

STEP 2

3 Divide the mixture between the 2
  prepared tins and level the surface.
Bake in the oven for 25 minutes, until
the cakes are well risen and feel springy
to the touch. Stand the tins on a wire
rack to cool, then turn the cakes out to
cool completely.

STEP 3

4 To make the filling, mix together
  the yogurt and icing
(confectioner's) sugar, then beat in the
lemon curd. Beat in a little more sifted
sugar if necessary, to make a stiff,
spreadable consistency.

STEP 4

5 Sandwich the 2 halves of the cake
  with the filling, and dust the top
with sifted icing (confectioner's) sugar.

STEP 5

STEP 1

STEP 2

STEP 3

STEP 4

SCOTTISH GINGERBREAD

This dark brown, spicy cake should be made well in advance of serving. It is best kept for at least 2 weeks, closely wrapped in foil.

SERVES 8
OVEN: 180°C/350°F/GAS 4

150 g/5 oz/1¼ cups wholewheat flour
½ tsp salt
2 tsp ground ginger
1 tsp ground cinnamon
grated nutmeg
2 tsp baking powder
175 g/6 oz/1 cup dark brown Muscovado
  sugar
150 g/5 oz/1⅓ cups rolled oats
6 tbsp black treacle (see below)
125 g/4 oz/½ cup butter
1 egg, beaten
150 ml/¼ pint/⅔ cup natural yogurt
125 g/4 oz/¾ cup sultanas
125 g/4 oz crystallized ginger, chopped
60 g/2 oz/½ cup blanched almond halves
about 150 ml/¼ pint/⅔ cup milk

1 Grease and line a 18 cm/7 in round cake tin (pan). Sift the flour, salt, ground ginger, cinnamon, nutmeg and baking powder into a bowl and tip in any bran remaining in the sieve. Stir in the sugar and rolled oats.

2 Put the treacle and butter into a small pan and warm it over low heat. Remove from the heat and stir with a wooden spoon to blend thoroughly.

3 Stir the butter mixture into the dry ingredients, then beat in the egg and yogurt. Stir in the sultanas and crystallized ginger. Stir in just enough milk to give a stiff, dropping consistency.

4 Spoon the mixture into the prepared tin (pan) and level the surface. Arrange the nuts over the surface. Bake in the preheated oven for 1½ hours, or until a fine skewer inserted in the centre of the cake comes out clean.

5 Leave the cake to cool in the tin (pan), then turn it out and stand on a wire rack to cool completely. Wrap closely in foil to store. Serve sliced, with yogurt cheese and honey, or with well-matured hard cheese and fresh fruit such as apples and pears.

BLACK TREACLE

An easy way to measure black treacle is to dip 2 tablespoons into boiling water until they are hot. Use one spoon to scoop out the treacle and the other to push it into the pan. Reheat the spoons as often as necessary.

PASSION CAKE

Decorating this moist, rich carrot cake with sugared flowers lifts it into the celebration class. It is a perfect choice for Easter.

STEP 1

STEP 3

STEP 4

STEP 5

SERVES 8-10
OVEN: 160°C/350°F/GAS 4

150 ml/¼ pint/²⁄₃ cup corn oil
175 g/6 oz/¾ cup golden caster sugar
4 tbsp natural yogurt
3 eggs, plus 1 extra yolk
1 tsp vanilla flavouring
125 g/4 oz/1 cup walnut pieces, chopped
175 g/6 oz carrots, grated
1 banana, mashed
175 g/ 6 oz/ 1½ cups flour
90 g/ 3 oz/¹⁄₂ cup fine oatmeal
1 tsp bicarbonate of soda
1 tsp baking powder
1 tsp ground cinnamon
½ tsp salt

FROSTING:
150 g/ 5 oz/ generous ½ cup yogurt cheese
   (see page 77), or low-fat soft cheese
4 tbsp natural yogurt
90 g/ 3 oz/¾ cup icing (confectioner's)
   sugar
1 tsp grated lemon rind
2 tsp lemon juice

DECORATION:
a few primroses and violets
45 g/ 1½ oz/ 3tbsp caster sugar
1 egg white, lightly beaten

1 Grease and line a 23 cm/9 in round cake tin (pan). Beat together the oil, sugar, yogurt, eggs, egg yolk and vanilla flavouring. Beat in the chopped walnuts, grated carrot and banana.

2 Sift together the remaining ingredients and gradually beat into the mixture.

3 Pour the mixture into the tin (pan) and level the surface. Bake in the preheated oven for 1½ hours, or until the cake is firm. To test, insert a fine skewer into the centre: it should come out clean. Leave to cool in the tin (pan) for 15 minutes, then turn out on a wire rack.

4 To make the frosting, beat together the cheese and yogurt. Sift in the icing (confectioner's) sugar and stir in the lemon rind and juice. Spread over the top and sides of the cake.

5 To prepare the decoration, dip the flowers quickly in the beaten egg white, then sprinkle with caster sugar to cover the surface completely. Place well apart on baking parchment. Leave in a warm, dry place for several hours until they are dry and crisp. Arrange the flowers in a pattern on top of the cake.

WHAT IS YOGURT?

NEW POTATO SALAD

SERVES 4

500 g/ 1 lb small new potatoes,
*   scrubbed*
salt
2 spring onions (scallions) thinly
*   sliced*
1 egg, hard-boiled and chopped

DRESSING:
2 tbsp natural yogurt
2 tbsp olive oil
1 tbsp red wine vinegar
large pinch of mustard powder
pepper

1. Cook the potatoes in boiling,
salted water until they are just
tender, then drain.

2. To make the dressing, beat
together the yogurt, oil,
vinegar and mustard powder
and season with salt and
pepper.

3. Pour the dressing over the
potatoes while they are still hot
and toss thoroughly. Set aside
to cool.

4. Stir the onion (scallions)
into the potato salad, transfer
to a serving dish and garnish it
with chopped hard-boiled egg.

No one knows who first invented yogurt,
or where in the world it was first
recognized as a healthy way of keeping
fresh milk beyond its normal use-by date.
It seems probable that it was discovered
by nomadic tribesmen crossing the vast
Asian continent, carrying fresh milk
from one camp to the next in primitive
bags made from the lining of sheep's
stomachs. Exposed to the heat of the sun
and not sterilized in any way, these
containers would have provided ideal
nursery conditions for the still-present
bacteria to grow.

Speculating again, it was probably only
a short step from the nomads' first taste
of this not-quite-sweet, not-quite-sour
dairy food to the discovery that a little of
yesterday's yogurt added to today's milk
will become tomorrow's fresh batch of
yogurt.

A taste for yogurt spread far beyond its
original homelands, and down the
centuries many claims have been made
for its beneficial properties, not least that
it is "the milk of eternal life".

In our own time yogurt is enjoyed for
its versatility and convenience. A tub of
yogurt in the refrigerator has the
makings of an instant snack or dessert; a
hasty sauce, salad dressing or dip; a
tenderizing marinade or coating and, as
our recipes show, a significant ingredient
in savoury dishes of all kinds.

More than that, yogurt offers the
consistency of a dairy product such as
cream or crème fraîche, with a much
lower fat content.

MAKING YOGURT

Although there is only one basic way of
making yogurt - by stirring hot milk
into a prepared yogurt culture or a
spoonful of starter from a previous batch
- there is enough scope for variation to
satisfy the most experimental cook. You
can use any combination of any kind of
milk from cows, goats or sheep,
skimmed or semi-skimmed, sterilized,
homogenized, pasteurized or
evaporated. For a luxurious-tasting
result you can make yogurt with a
proportion of single cream and milk,
and for a thicker product you can stir 1
tablespoon of powdered milk into
whatever milk you use.

Yogurt culture is made with either
Lactobacillus bulgaricus or *Lactobacillus
acidopholus*, which develop most readily
when the milk is added at a temperature
between 32°- 40°C/90°-120°F and is
allowed to cool to a constant
temperature no lower than 18°C/65°F
for the 8 hours it takes the yogurt to set.

Primitive and non-scientific methods
of achieving this included putting the
maturing yogurt in a covered container
inside a "hay box" cooker, or in a
specially padded and insulated tin, on a
tray in the warming drawer of an oven
or in the airing cupboard. If you want to
eliminate the element of chance, you
can use an electric yogurt-making
appliance which is thermostatically
controlled to keep the developing
culture at the correct temperature.

YOGURT

To make 1 litre/1¾ pints/4 cups

1 litre/ 1 ¹/₄ pints/ 4 cups milk
1 tbsp plain yogurt, or a sachet of
commercial culture

1. Pour the milk into a pan and, unless it has already been sterilized, bring it to the boil, then turn off the heat. Allow it to cool until, when you dip in a clean finger, you can keep it in the milk without discomfort while you count slowly to 10. If the milk is sterilized you need only heat it to 32°-40°C/90°-120°F.

2. Put the starter yogurt in a small bowl, pour on a little of the milk and beat it thoroughly.

3. Pour the yogurt mixture into the milk remaining in the pan and stir to blend it thoroughly.

4. Pour the milk mixture into a scrupulously clean container such as an earthenware or heat-proof glass bowl, a number of small containers or a yogurt maker.

5. Cover the containers and set aside in a warm place, without disturbing them, for 8-10 hours. The longer you leave the culture in the warmth, the more acidic it will become and the more the flavour will sharpen.

6. Transfer the yogurt to the refrigerator, and remember to save at least 1 tablespoon to start the next batch.

Storing yogurt

Yogurt continues to change its character even in the chill temperature of a refrigerator. You can store it, in a covered container, for up to seven days, but by then it may start to separate and will have developed a sharp, tangy flavour. It is best to use some to make your next batch of yogurt before it reaches that stage. Home-made yogurt does not freeze satisfactorily, and frozen yogurt cannot be used as a starter.

Stabilizing yogurt

If you plan to use yogurt in a recipe which involves adding cold yogurt to a hot liquid, or in which the yogurt will be brought to boiling point, it is best to stabilize it first, to prevent separation. The way to do this, using cornflour (cornstarch) to thicken it, is described on page 12. Although separation will not affect the flavour of the dish, it does spoil the texture and appearance.

Do not use stabilized yogurt as a starter to make another batch. The high temperature at which it is stirred will kill the bacteria.

YOGURT CHEESE

Once you are in the habit of making your own yogurt, or if you buy yogurt in reasonably large quantities, the next step is to make your own soft cheese. You can use it in place of cottage cheese or commercially made low-fat soft cheese in sandwiches and snacks, salads and toppings, baked dishes and desserts.

The yield varies slightly according to the type of milk from which the yogurt

CHOCOLATE CHIP COOKIES

Makes about 26
Oven:190°C/375°F/Gas 5

90 g/ 3 oz/6 tbsp unsalted butter,
softened
60 g/ 2 oz/¹/₄ cup caster sugar
90 g/ 3 oz/¹/₂ cup light
Muscovado sugar
1 egg, lightly beaten
175 g/6 oz/1 ¹/₂ cups self-raising
(all-purpose) flour
pinch of salt
¹/₂ tsp vanilla flavouring
90 g/ 3 oz plain chocolate,
chopped

1. Brush 2 baking sheets with vegetable oil. Beat the butter and sugar until the mixture is thick and creamy. Beat in the egg, then stir in the flour, salt, vanilla and chocolate pieces.

2. Drop teaspoon-sized heaps of the mixture well apart on to the prepared baking trays. Bake in the preheated oven for 12-15 minutes until the cookies are golden brown. Transfer to a wire rack to cool, then store in an airtight tin.

CHOCOLATE CARAQUE

Spread the chocolate pieces on a large plate over a pan of simmering water until melted, then use a palette knife to spread it on a cool surface. When cool, scrape it into curls by drawing a sharp knife blade firmly across the surface.

SPICED COURGETTES (ZUCCHINI)

4 tbsp vegetable oil
3 medium courgettes (zucchini), sliced
250 ml/ 8 fl oz/ 1 cup natural yogurt
2 garlic cloves, crushed
½ tsp cumin seeds, lightly crushed
pinch of chilli powder
large pinch of paprika
salt

1. Heat the oil in a frying pan and fry the courgettes (zucchini), in a single layer, until light brown on all sides. Transfer to a warmed dish.

2. Place the yogurt in a bowl, stir in the garlic, cumin seeds and chilli powder and season. Just before serving, pour over the courgettes (zucchini) and sprinkle with paprika.

CLARIFIED BUTTER

To clarify butter, place 125 g/ 4 oz/½ cup unsalted butter in a small pan. Melt the butter over low heat, then strain into a bowl. Discard the sediment that collects at the base of the pan.

was made, and the length of time it was left to drain. As a guide, any quantity of yogurt will provide just over half its volume in yogurt cheese. The whey that is drained off can be stored in the refrigerator and used in place of stock in soups and sauces.

To make 400 g/14 oz/1½ cups Cheese

1 litre/ 1¾ pints/ 4 cups natural yogurt
salt (optional)

1. Line a colander with a double thickness of cheesecloth or muslin. Tip in the yogurt and draw the muslin over to cover it. Or tie the corners of the muslin to make a bag. Stand the colander in a bowl, or hang the bag over a bowl, to catch the whey.

2. Leave it to drain overnight. Transfer the yogurt to a bowl and, if you wish, beat in a little salt. Store in a covered container in the refrigerator for up to a week.

Storing yogurt cheese

You may like to store some of your yogurt cheese in the traditional Middle Eastern way. Scoop out small spoonfuls and roll them into walnut-sized balls. Pack them in a lidded jar and pour on olive oil to cover the cheese completely. Add any flavourings you wish, such as bay leaves, sprigs of thyme or rosemary, dried chillies, peppercorns or mustard seeds.

To serve, lift out the cheese as required with a draining spoon, drain off the excess oil and roll the balls in chopped walnuts. Serve these cheese balls with cocktail sticks, as an appetizer with drinks.

YOGURT DRINKS

Sweet or salty, chilled and tingling with ice, yogurt drinks are deeply rooted in Middle Eastern and Indian cuisines. And now, increasingly, their popularity is spreading as more of us wake up to the news that a long, cool glass of yogurt-plus is as refreshing and revitalizing as an early morning cup of tea or coffee.

You can make a jug of Ayran or Lassi overnight and chill it to serve in an instant in the morning; serve it before a spicy meal to prepare the palate for the medley of flavours to come, or as an accompaniment to an Indian meal, when the contrast of bland and spicy, hot and cold elements will be specially pleasing.

You can also add your own combination of fruits and syrups, cereals and nuts until you have a nutritious meal in a glass; just the thing for anyone who takes breakfast at the double, or for serving to children who refuse a "proper" breakfast.

AYRAN

This is the favourite soft drink of Turkey and other Middle Eastern countries, where it is sold, refreshingly chilled, by street sellers.

Serves 2

300 ml/½ pint/ 1¼ cups natural yogurt, chilled
300 ml/½ pint/ 1¼ cups water, chilled
½ tsp salt
½ tsp dried mint, or 1 tsp chopped fresh mint
ice cubes, to serve
mint sprigs, to garnish (optional)

Whisk together the yogurt and water and stir in the salt and mint. Store in a covered container in the refrigerator if it is not to be served at once.

To serve, add ice cubes and, if you wish, a sprig of mint, and serve in chilled glasses, with straws.

LASSI

Some Indian restaurant menus offer a salt drink similar to Ayran, or a sweet version, which may include any combination of nuts, chopped dried fruits, desiccated coconut and food colouring. This is refreshing for "elevenses", too.

SERVES 2

300 ml/ 1/2 pint/ 1 1/4 cups natural yogurt,
  chilled
300 ml/ 1/2 pint/ 1 1/4 cups milk, chilled
1 tsp rosewater or orange-flower water
2 tsp desiccated coconut
1 tbsp seedless raisins
2 tsp caster sugar
ice cubes, to serve
ground cinnamon, to sprinkle (optional)

Whisk together the yogurt, milk and rosewater or orange-flower water and stir in the coconut, raisins and sugar. Pour into two tall, chilled glasses, add the ice cubes and, if you wish, sprinkle a little ground cinnamon on top. Serve chilled, with straws and long-handled spoons.

BANANA COOLER

This "meal-in-a-glass" is especially good at breakfast-time.

SERVES 2

300 ml/ 1/2 pint/ 1 1/4 cups natural yogurt,
  chilled
1 tbsp clear honey
2 small bananas, chopped
1 tbsp muesli
ground cinnamon, to sprinkle (optional)

Put the yogurt, honey and bananas into a blender or food processor, and process until smooth. Divide the mixture between 2 glasses and sprinkle each one with muesli and, if you wish, ground cinnamon. Serve with straws and long-handled spoons.

FRUIT WHIP

A frothy yogurt version of a milkshake.

SERVES 4

300 ml/ 1/2 pint/ 1 1/4 cups natural yogurt,
  chilled
300 ml/ 1/2 pint/ 1 1/4 cups fruit purée, such as
  strawberry, raspberry, apple, or dried
  apricot, chilled
1 tbsp clear honey
1 egg white, stiffly beaten
fresh fruit or herb sprays, to decorate

Whisk together the yogurt, fruit purée and honey. Fold in the egg white and divide between 4 glasses. Decorate with fruit or a herbal spray. Serve with straws.

FLAVOURING YOGURT

Whether you make your own yogurt or buy large cartons of plain yogurt in the supermarket, it is rewarding to have your own repertoire of flavourings, which will soon become family favourites.

Sweet flavourings
- Crumbled chocolate flake and chopped hazelnuts
- Fresh strawberries and strawberry syrup
- Chopped orange segments with concentrated orange juice and grated orange rind
- Chopped Turkish delight and a sprinkling of rosewater
- Clear honey and a few pomegranate seeds
- Chopped dates and blanched almonds
- Chopped stewed dried apricots and apricot brandy

Savoury Blends
These savoury blends can be served as sauces and as appetizing dips, with crisps, crackers or crudités:

- Chopped watercress and chopped macadamia nuts, with a dash of lemon juice
- Mayonnaise, chopped hard-boiled egg and snipped chives
- Mayonnaise, capers, chopped green pepper and snipped spring onion tops
- Lumpfish roe, lemon juice and chopped parsley
- Grated horseradish, double cream and chopped mint

INDEX